Three Ame

Heroes

by Guadalupe V. Lopez

Table of Contents

Introduction

What is a hero? A hero is a person who makes the world a better place. Here are three American heroes. They are real people who made the United States a better place for everyone.

Jane Addams lived from 1860 to 1935.

Martin Luther King, Jr. lived from 1929 to 1968.

César Chávez lived from 1927 to 1993.

Chapter 1

Who Was Jane Addams?

Jane Addams had a good life. Her family had plenty of money. She felt that others should live well, too. Her idea was simple. She wanted everyone to have a good life.

Jane Addams dreamed of making life better for all people.

Many immigrants lived in crowded spaces.

Addams was born in 1860. Her family lived in a nice house. One day, she saw a poor part of the city. Many **immigrants** lived there. Houses were falling apart. Children had torn clothes.

Addams was just a girl, but she wanted to help. She wanted to change the way poor people lived.

In 1889, Addams' found a big house and filled it with pretty things. She called it Hull House.

Addams gave classes to immigrants. They came from different cultures. They spoke different languages. At Hull House, they could learn to speak and read English, do math, and other things, too.

Hull House had a day care and a kindergarten. ➲

Today Hull House is a museum.

In 1931, Jane Addams received the **Nobel Peace Prize** for helping so many people. Today, the Hull House Association still helps people.

Chapter 2

Who Was Martin Luther King, Jr.?

Years ago, white people and black people in America were not treated the same. Martin Luther King, Jr., wanted to change this.

King was born in 1929, in Atlanta, Georgia. At that time, whites and blacks were kept apart. In some places, this was the law.

King knew that the law was wrong and fought for change. But he fought for **civil rights** with his words, not his fists. He dreamed of the same rights for all citizens of the United States.

On August 28, 1963, Dr. King gave a famous speech in Washington, D.C. It was called "I Have a Dream."

In this photo, President Lyndon Johnson is signing the Civil Rights Act. It gave African Americans the same rights as other citizens.

King gave speeches and led marches. These actions changed our country. In 1964, King received the Nobel Peace Prize.

Sadly, King was killed in 1968. Today, Americans celebrate his birthday on January 15. We honor Martin Luther King, Jr. by helping others. We can make the world better too.

Chapter 3

Who Was César Chávez?

César Chávez was born in Yuma, Arizona, in 1927. His father had a small farm. Their relatives lived nearby.

When Chávez was ten, there was not enough rain. Crops died. The Chávez family lost their farm.

César Chávez dreamed that workers would be treated well and have a better life. ➲

Many migrant camps did not have water.

The family moved to California. They became **migrant** workers. They went from farm to farm picking crops. They never stayed in one place. Chávez went to more than 30 different schools.

Chávez left school after eighth grade. He picked grapes with his family. They made pennies a day. A family could not live on so little money.

Migrants worked many hours for very little pay.

A grape grower signs a contract. He is agreeing to pay workers more money.

Chávez wanted things to change. He became a leader for the migrant workers. In 1968 Chávez asked people all over the United States not to buy grapes. Grape growers lost money. They finally agreed to treat workers better.

Chávez died in 1993. In 1994, President Clinton honored Chávez by awarding him the Presidential Medal of Freedom.

Conclusion

Jane Addams, Martin Luther King, Jr., and César Chávez were ordinary Americans. They lived at different times and in different places. They came from different cultures.

But with words and deeds, these three American heroes improved the lives of many people. They changed our country forever.

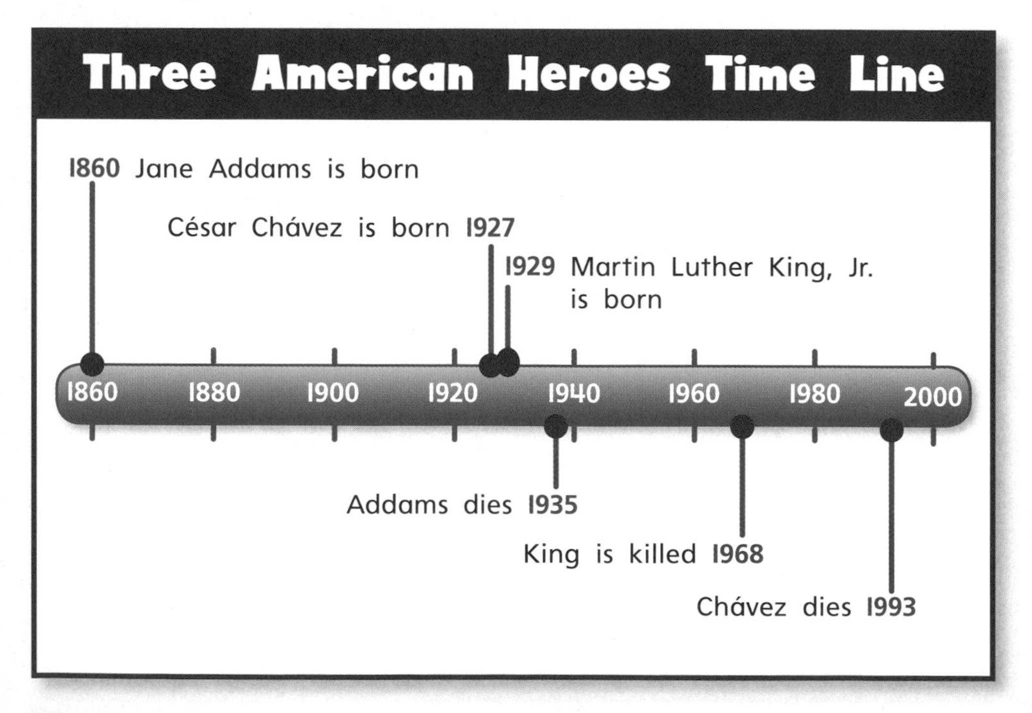

Glossary

Civil Rights *(SI-vuhl reyets)* freedoms that all people enjoy by law ***(page 8)***

immigrants *(IM-uh-grents)* people who move from one country to another ***(page 4)***

migrant *(MEYE-gruhnt)* going from place to place ***(page 11)***

Nobel Peace Prize *(NOH-bel Pees Preyez)* prize given to someone who makes the world a better place ***(page 6)***

Index

Comprehension Check

Retell

Use a Main Idea and Details chart to retell the information in this book.

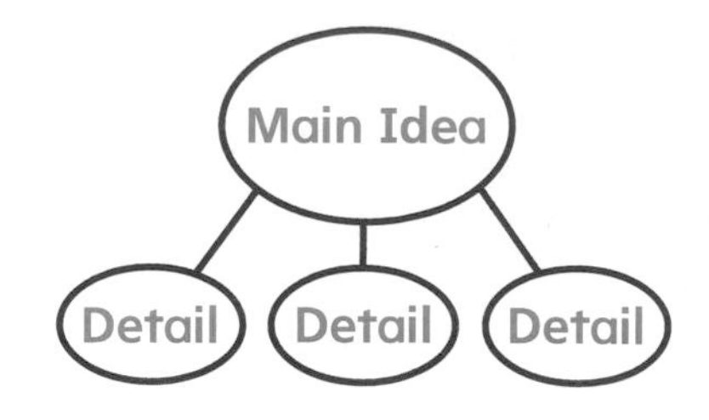

Think and Compare

1. Jane Addams wanted everyone to have a good life. How did Addams help make this happen? ***(Main Idea and Details)***

2. How were Chávez's ideas like King's ideas? ***(Synthesize)***

3. Martin Luther King Day of Service is in January. What can you do to help someone on this day? ***(Apply)***